EDUCATOR, FEMINIST, AND ANTI-LYNCHING CIVIL RIGHTS LEADER

# IDA B. WELLS, VOICE OF TRUTH

WRITTEN BY
**MICHELLE DUSTER**

ILLUSTRATED BY
**LAURA FREEMAN**

**GODWINBOOKS**

Henry Holt and Company
New York

T0037050

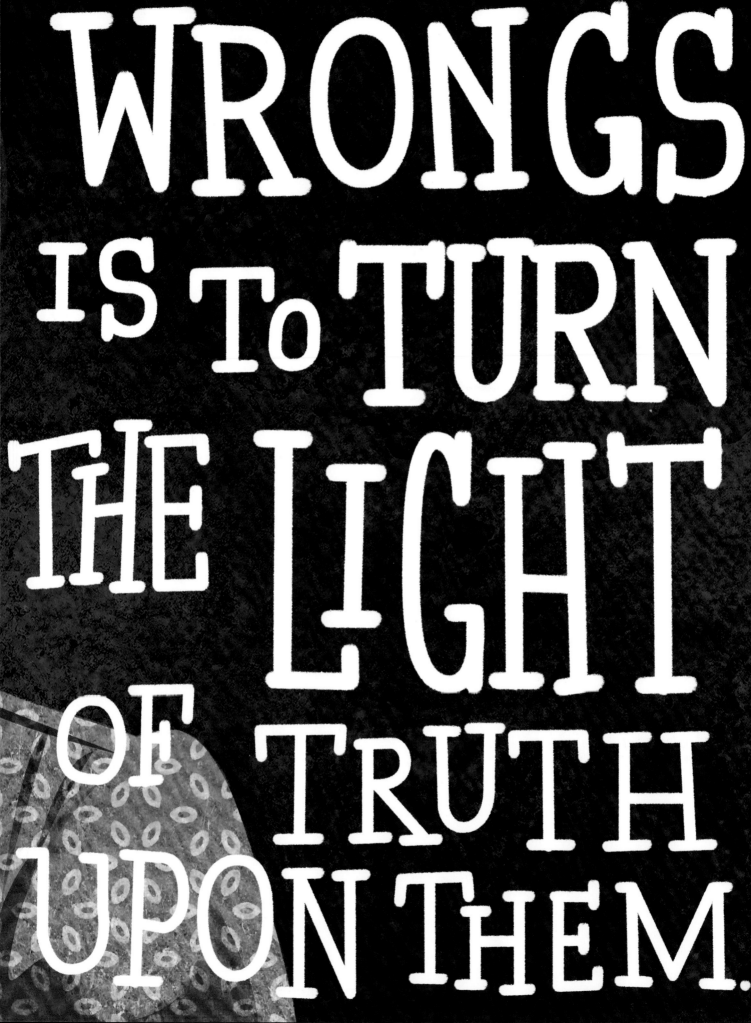

To the next generation of leaders:
May you always be willing to stand in your own truth.
—M. D.

For my mom Trudy, and for
all the other brave women everywhere.
—L. F.

Henry Holt and Company, *Publishers since 1866*
Henry Holt® is a registered trademark of Macmillan Publishing Group, LLC
120 Broadway, New York, NY 10271 • mackids.com

Text copyright © 2022 by Michelle Duster. Illustrations copyright © 2022 by Laura Freeman.
All rights reserved.

Our books may be purchased in bulk for promotional, educational, or business use.
Please contact your local bookseller or the Macmillan Corporate and Premium Sales Department
at (800) 221-7945 ext. 5442 or by email at MacmillanSpecialMarkets@macmillan.com.

Library of Congress Cataloging-in-Publication Data is available.

First edition, 2022
Book design by Jen Keenan
The art for this book was created digitally in Photoshop.
Printed in China by RR Donnelley Asia Printing Solutions Ltd.,
Dongguan City, Guangdong Province

ISBN 978-1-250-23946-4 (hardcover)
3 5 7 9 10 8 6 4 2

Some people refer to my great-grandmother Ida B. Wells as a "boss." She was an educator, a journalist, a feminist, a businesswoman, a newspaper owner, a public speaker, a suffragist, a civil rights activist, and a women's club leader.

She was a founder of the National Association for the Advancement of Colored People (NAACP), a founder of the National Association of Colored Women's Clubs (NACWC), a founder of the Alpha Suffrage Club, and a founder of the Negro Fellowship League.

She wrote.

She spoke.

She traveled.

She challenged the racist and sexist norms of her time that often involved violence and terror.

Although she endured enormous criticism and threats to her life, she never gave up.

She fought for equality and justice for almost fifty years.

Ida B. Wells was born into slavery in Holly Springs, Mississippi, on July 16, 1862.

At just sixteen years old, Ida lost both of her parents and a younger brother in a yellow fever epidemic. Even though she was just a teenager, she assumed the enormous responsibility of taking care of her five remaining siblings.

She started her career as a
teacher in rural Mississippi,

then moved to Memphis,
where she continued to teach.

Ida also began writing for church newsletters.
She wrote about social and political issues at the time.

One day in 1884, when Ida was in her early twenties, she was riding a train when the conductor asked her to move from the "ladies' car" to the "colored car," which doubled as the smoking car. She refused and was thrown off the train.

Rather than cower to the powers that be, she wrote about the incident in the newspaper and sued the Chesapeake, Ohio & Southwestern Railroad. She won the case and was awarded $500, though it was appealed all the way to the Tennessee Supreme Court.

Almost two and a half years later, the ruling was overturned in favor of the railroad, and Ida B. Wells was accused of harassing the company.

While still teaching, Ida became co-owner of the *Memphis Free Speech* newspaper and built up a following as a writer. She expressed her frustration with separate and unequal school systems and wrote about it—then lost her teaching job. So Ida got busy traveling around the area selling subscriptions for the newspaper.

My great-grandmother's life completely changed on March 9, 1892.
Three of her enterprising friends who owned a grocery store, which
rivaled a white-owned store, were lynched.

Ida B. Wells knew that her friends—Thomas Moss, Calvin McDowell, and William Stewart—were only guilty of being economic rivals to a white-owned business.

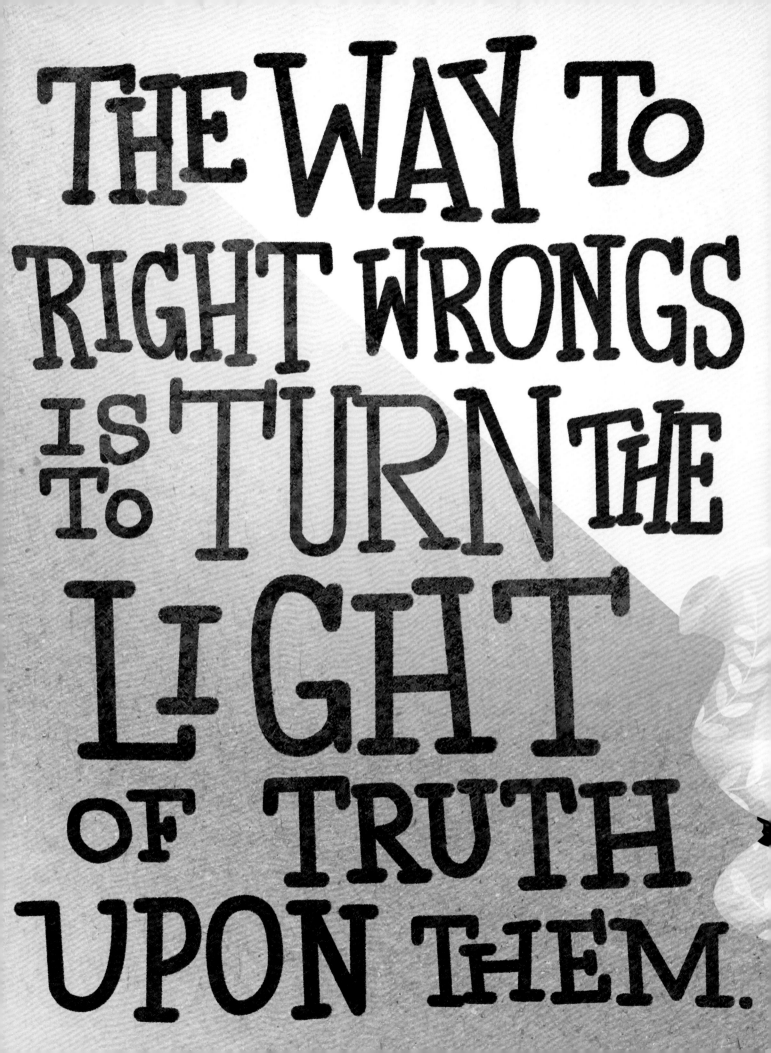

THE WAY TO RIGHT WRONGS IS TO TURN THE LIGHT OF TRUTH UPON THEM.

At the time, the common narrative to justify lynching was that Black men violated white women, but Ida recognized that the murder of her friends had nothing to do with that crime. She realized lynching was used to keep the Black community in an economically and socially inferior position.

Ida exposed the truth about why her friends were lynched, urging Black people in Memphis to boycott streetcars and white-owned businesses and to pack up their stuff and head to Oklahoma (which was a territory at the time).

Even though the people from the streetcar company warned her to stop, Ida continued to speak out.

Mrs Ida B Wells

A LECTURE

While she was out of town in Philadelphia, her printing press was destroyed and she was threatened to be killed on sight. She lost everything she owned and never returned to Memphis.

Ida went on to New York City, where she worked with T. Thomas Fortune on his *New York Age* newspaper. She wrote pamphlets about the reality of lynching and started speaking publicly about its horrors, both in the United States and abroad.

In 1895, she married attorney and newspaper owner Ferdinand L. Barnett and did what few married women did at that time: she hyphenated her last name, becoming Ida B. Wells-Barnett.

She and her husband had four children together;
their youngest daughter, Alfreda, is my grandmother.

Ida B. Wells-Barnett was involved in the suffrage movement.

She started the first kindergarten for Black children in Chicago and worked to stop the racial segregation of schools.

She founded and managed the Negro Fellowship League, which provided housing and job assistance to Black men who migrated to Chicago from the South.

Wherever she saw injustice or inequality, Ida raised
her voice and did what she could to effect change.
She died at age sixty-eight on March 25, 1931.

Ida B. Wells spent her life fighting for justice and equality. She truly believed that exposing injustice would lead to change. "The way to right wrongs is to turn the light of truth upon them," she said. Even in the face of threats and criticism, she refused to be silent.

She refused to make herself small.
She stood up. Spoke out.
And she made a difference for us all.

# Ida B. Wells: A Life

1862   Ida Bell Wells born in Holly Springs, Mississippi, on July 16

1878   Both parents and younger brother died in yellow fever epidemic

1883   Removed from Chesapeake, Ohio & Southwestern Railroad ladies' car on trip from Memphis to Woodstock on September 15

1884   Removed from train car on trip from Woodstock to Memphis on May 4, sued railroad and won in Shelby County Circuit Court

1887   Lawsuit overturned by Tennessee Supreme Court

1889   Became co-owner of *Memphis Free Speech*

1891   Lost teaching job, put all her energy into growing the newspaper

1892   Ida's friends were lynched. She wrote articles, her life was threatened, and she was exiled from the South. Worked with T. Thomas Fortune on the *New York Age* and published *Southern Horrors: Lynch Law in All Its Phases.*

1893   Traveled on speaking tour in Great Britain. Wrote, edited, and published pamphlet *The Reason Why the Colored American Is Not in the World's Columbian Exposition,* which she distributed at the World's Fair in Chicago.

1894   Went on four-month speaking tour in England

1895   Published *A Red Record: Tabulated Statistics and Alleged Causes of Lynching in the United States, 1892–1893–1894.* On June 27, married Ferdinand L. Barnett at Bethel AME Church in Chicago, settled in the city, and had four children between 1896 and 1904.

1896   Cofounded National Association of Colored Women's Clubs

1897   Established first kindergarten for Black children in Chicago

1899   Wrote *Lynch Law in Georgia* pamphlet

1900   Wrote *Mob Rule in New Orleans* pamphlet

1909   Cofounded NAACP in response to 1908 riot in Springfield, IL

1910  Started Negro Fellowship League, which
       she managed until it closed in 1920
1913  Founded the Alpha Suffrage Club and
       helped Oscar De Priest get elected in
       1914 as first African American alderman
       in Chicago. Marched in Washington,
       DC, and Chicago, IL, suffrage parades.
1917  Wrote *The East St. Louis Massacre* pamphlet
1920  Visited Elaine, Arkansas, sharecroppers in prison
       and wrote *The Arkansas Race Riot* pamphlet
1930  Ran and lost race for Illinois state senate
1931  Ida B. Wells-Barnett died from kidney failure on March 25.

In the years following Ida B. Wells's death, there have been many tributes and honors. In her adopted city of Chicago, there was a substantial housing community called the Ida B. Wells Homes, which housed thousands of people from 1941 to 2002. There is a major downtown street renamed Ida B. Wells Drive, an honorary Ida B. Wells Way, and a historical marker near her house, which is a registered historic landmark. And a committee worked tirelessly for over thirteen years to have an Ida B. Wells Monument installed on the land where the Ida B. Wells Homes once stood.

In her hometown of Holly Springs, there is a post office named after her, an Ida B. Wells-Barnett Museum, and a historical marker in the town square. The city of Memphis honored her with a historical marker, included her in a monument to suffragists, and created a statue of her on Beale Street.

Ida B. Wells has been featured on a US Black Heritage postage stamp, and many awards, organizations, and schools have been named after her. She has been inducted into many halls of fame and was awarded a posthumous Pulitzer Prize Special Citation in 2020. Her autobiography was edited by her daughter and published in 1970, and her great-granddaughter edited two books of Ida's writing and wrote a book about her life and legacy, which was published in 2021. Her legacy lives on through dozens of descendants as well as the efforts of many around the country who honor her and teach about her through books, films, lectures, plays, exhibits, tours, and more.

THE PEOPLE MUST KNOW BEFORE THEY CAN ACT, AND THERE IS NO EDUCATOR TO COMPARE WITH THE PRESS.